Prayers of a Needy One

Reflections on the Spiritual Journey

Curt McKee

Prayers of a Needy One: Reflections on the Spiritual Journey
ISBN: Softcover 978-1-955581-82-0
Copyright © 2022 by Curt McKee

Parson's Porch Books is an imprint of Parson's Porch *&* Company (PP*&*C) in Cleveland, Tennessee. PP*&*C is an innovative organization which raises money by publishing books of noted authors, representing all genres.

Parson's Porch *&* Company *turns books into bread & milk* by sharing its profits with the poor.

www.parsonsporch.com

Prayers of a Needy One

Take. Breathe.

Take these One Hundred Days
of reflective breath prayers
and thoughts, allowing them to
strengthen you in your journey
with Jesus Christ.

Day One

Philippians 2:3-5

Mark 8:34

Deliver me, O Lord from the me which would pull away from You. Let me be ever closer to You.

Day Two

Matthew 7:1-5

Keep me, O Lord from that spirit
within, which bids me to notice
the sins of others while ignoring
my own. Especially keep me from
correcting others while minimizing
my own struggle with the sinful
nature.

Day Three

Romans 3:23

I John 1:8-10

Grant me dear Lord, never to fail
to estimate my own brokenness,
fallenness, and sinful pull before
daring assess that of anyone else.

Day Four

Ephesians 4:26-27

God, hold me back from anger
that is merely a response for not
getting what I desire. Help me to
be only angry at blatant
unrighteousness yet to do so
always in a spirit of grace and
humility.

Day Five

John 1:4, 9 8:12

Matthew 5:14-16

In my dark moments, O Lord, teach me to look only for Your Light. All others will be mere multiplications of darkness no matter how much they resemble light.

Day Six

Mark 3:35

Forgive me, Lord, in the times I might easily forget that every person I meet is a potential child of Yours and thus a sister or brother of mine.

Day Seven

Philippians 2:3-4

Galatians 2:6

Matthew 10:7-8

Lord, help me be reminded that Your blessings are never to be for me alone but are manifested in me so as to become blessings for others. Philippians 2:3-4 Galatians 2:6 Matthew 10:7-8

Day Eight

I Peter 2:9

I Thessalonians 5:5

Deliver me, O God, from my own
darkness so that I might be Your
most wondrous light for others.

Day Nine

Proverbs 21:13

Lord, give me always the ability to move beyond my me-pull. For it is only then that I will be enabled to hear the needy cries of those around me.

Day Ten

Mark 8:34-35; 10:44-45

Lord, show the true path of self-emptying which You walked on this earth. For it is only in emptying myself of me that I can be more full of You.

Day Eleven

James 4:4

Galatians 5:24

O Lord, let me walk ever closer with You. Let me stay more in step with Your Spirit even when I become more out of step with the world.

Day Twelve

John 13:34-35

I Peter 3:13-14, 16

God of my heart, keep me from allowing my hurt, my pain to cause such responses from me that bring hurt and pain to others. For if I truly desire a life of love, then love must be the measure of my pursuits even when I suffer.

Day Thirteen

Psalm 139:14

John 15:15

Lord, help me to continually see myself not as I wish myself to be, not even as I may prefer that others wish for me to be. Help me to see me as You see me, through lenses of love revealed in Your Son. Psalm 139:14 John 15:15

Day Fourteen

Mark 14:66-72

Lord, remind me that in being not
ashamed of the gospel, I shame a
lesser part within me which like
Peter (Simon) could deny even
knowing the Savior.

Day Fifteen

Proverbs 16:18

Lord, deliver me from prideful
moments wherein I feel my sins
and weaknesses are not as
offensive as those of others.

Day Sixteen

Galatians 1:10

Acts 4:19-20

Lord, keep me from those times when I am more concerned with what others think or what I myself desire than what I know You need from me.

Day Seventeen

Proverbs 16:9

Lord, deliver me from those seasons
I take on myself to believe what I
desire of my life is superior to what
You have revealed I should be.

Day Eighteen

Genesis 28:16

Psalm 139:7

Dear Lord, hold me fast in the
numb times when not only can I
not feel for others but am so
stricken, I feel I cannot discern
You. Help me be certain, you
really are there. Genesis 28:16
Psalm 139:7

Day Nineteen

I Samuel 16:7

Lord, deliver me from that part
which seeks never to find good in
those who are different from me.
Help me look, really look, to the
deeper places wherein I know
Your image lies no Matthewer
how contrary the outward
evidence may be.

Day Twenty

Matthew 7:3-5

Lord, deliver me from spiritual blindness which is so prevalent that I see sin in others oblivious to its presence in me. May all sin fade from view when the cross, the wondrous cross, comes fully into focus.

Day Twenty-One

Acts 11:24

Lord, keep me from that tendency
to be so full of me I that I fail to
see how emptied I become of
You.

Day Twenty-Two

Matthew 11:28-30

II Corinthians 12:10

Lord, help me in all weary
moments to be reminded that
when I am in You, my weakness
displays Your perfect strength.

Day Twenty-Three

Luke 9:23

Galatians 6:14

Lord, help me always remember a cross was required to pay for my sin; a cross was taken by an innocent man for the sake of my sin; and a cross is required if I will walk in the way of the Savior.

Day Twenty-Four

Romans 5:20-21

Lord, help me balance my
understanding so as to realize my
struggles continue to remind me
of the greatness of Your grace,
Your strength.

Day Twenty-Five

Philippians 4:13

Lord, keep ever in my thoughts
these words; I can do nothing in
my own strength. I can do all
things in Yours.

Day Twenty-Six

Psalm 51:17

Lord, may I never shrink from having my heart broken by the things that break Yours. Psalm 51:17

Day Twenty-Seven

Psalm 46:10

I Kings 19:12

Lord, continue to teach me that
even when voices of the culture
scream loudly, abounding with
limitless activity and busy
movement, I can rest in You
alone. I can still myself and hear
Your gentle whisper which is how
the Spirit often speaks to me.

Day Twenty-Eight

Psalm 19:14

Lord, may the passion within for You never be diminished by outward passion of others, even when their passions are not evil yet do not fully reflect who You are. May I become all You need me to be inside and outside.

Day Twenty-Nine

I Thessalonians 5:1-18

Psalm 118:1

Lord, teach me never to be so hasty that I miss great opportunities for gratitude to rise up in my heart and be expressed by my life.

Day Thirty

John 1:14

Wonderful Savior, teach me to never fail at beholding Your true majesty and greatness. Help me to ever hold You in awe and respect from the depths of my heart. John 1:14

Day Thirty-One

Colossians 2:13-14

John 11:25-26

Lord, preserve me from any motivation which makes me no longer marvel at Your love for me. The cross is marvelous. The resurrection is marvelous. The grace which applies Christ's cross and resurrection to me, is marvelous!

Day Thirty-Two

Hebrews 4:7

II Corinthians 4:18

I John 2:15-17

Lord deliver me from a hard-heartedness in the midst of troubling days and from any personal views which are shaped by anything which is not from Your revealed truth. Keep me from all attitudes, words, and attention given to things which in the eternal, matter little, if at all.

Day Thirty-Three

Romans 5:19-21 12:6

Lord, help me always remember that the grace I receive is to be both held in my heart and shared with others, especially those who hardly know the way of grace.

Day Thirty-Four

Romans 3:21-24 5:6-8

Lord, may I never forget that I am but a sinner redeemed and still being redeemed by the power of Your grace. My part is minimal but is a part. Your role, once more shows You are a God of love.

Day Thirty-Five

John 16:33

Lord, the "trouble" You mentioned we would have in the world often overwhelms. Help me to recall the conclusion You drew regarding this so that I may "be of good cheer" knowing You have overcome the world with all its troubling aspects.

Day Thirty-Six

Psalm 119:105

Lord, remind me that light for my journey includes only the next step or next few steps along the way. In Your keeping, remains all further steps and their results.

Day Thirty-Seven

John 11:25

Luke 24:6-7

Lord, let me ever be pulled by the life that comes through the resurrection of Jesus Christ. May this be especially true when to acquire this life requires the death of any part of me.

Day Thirty-Eight

John 14:13

Acts 3:16

Philippians 2:9-10

Lord, help me always keep in sight that in his name, in Jesus' name, I find the nature that brings salvation, healing, deliverance and all things necessary for a holy life.

Day Thirty-Nine

I Peter 1:16

Hebrews 12:14

Lord, keep me ever mindful that to be holy never infers I am better that others, only that I am better than I could ever be without the power and presence of Christ.

Day Forty

I Corinthians 2:9-10

Luke 8:17

Lord, help me never to be so enamored with the great questions of life, which You have chosen not to fully reveal, that I might miss important "along the way" answers which have been clearly revealed. I Corinthians 2:9-10 Luke 8:17

Day Forty-One

Romans 5:20-21

Ephesians 2:5

Lord, as I ponder the sinfulness of humanity, I marvel at how Your love could never be thwarted by sin. In fact, Your love in Jesus Christ, did everything necessary to enable us to overcome sin.

Day Forty-Two

Matthew 5:44-45

I Corinthians 13:13

Lord of my heart, remind me that love comes first in all my relationships, including especially, relationships with those who are not easily loved.

Day Forty-Three

Psalm 139:7

Matthew 28:20

Lord, help me underscore the importance of Your presence. May I never forget You are only a prayer away.

Day Forty-Four

Matthew 25:40

Lord, help me see Jesus in the least, the last, in the poor, the hungry, the diseased. For then it will be most difficult for me to take their plight lightly.

Day Forty-Five

Proverbs 19:17

Matthew 5:42

Lord, give me the grace to not turn away the needy but to open my heart to Your plan for ways I can bring comfort to their lives.

Day Forty-Six

Mark 4:39-40

Lord, in the midst of storms be the calm and whisper peace to the very depths of my soul.

Day Forty-Seven

Galatians 6:14

Lord, teach me never to boast in myself, in any human or human effort; only in the cross of Christ Jesus which completely alters my existence.

Day Forty-Eight

Psalm 19:14

I Thessalonians 2:4

Lord, may I desire only what truly pleases You even when it brings me inconvenience and is not pleasing to those who are nearby or ones who are a part of my life.

Day Forty-Nine

Colossians 1:12

II Corinthians 5:18

Lord, offenses may come from those who do not understand Your ways, nor understand my efforts to walk in them. Let me never face such times with anything less than gratitude that I am worthy to relate to Your Son even when I am misunderstood. Colossians 1:12 II Corinthians 5:18

Day Fifty

Ephesians 5:15-17

Lord, help me place less emphasis on my being understood and be more concerned for my own understanding of Your desire and design for my life.

Day Fifty-One

Psalm 119:105

Jeremiah 1:7

Lord, guide my steps and my stops as I travel this amazing journey with You. Fill me with Your Spirit daily and guide me with Your Word.

Day Fifty-Two

Romans 6:12-14

I John 1:8-10

Lord, help me find more offense in the sin with which I struggle than with any I may behold in the lives of others. Teach me to be so permeated by the Spirit of Your Son that sin never has dominion in my life.

Day Fifty-Three

John 1:12-13

I John 3:1-2

O God, keep me ever humbled at the thought that I am Your child. Through Christ I am born anew into Your family. John 1:12-13 I John 3:1-2

Day Fifty-Four

Matthew 5:16; 10:7-8

Dear Lord, help me always to remember that I am never blessed merely for my own sake but that Your blessings might somehow flow through me into the lives of others. Matthew 5:16 10:7-8

Day Fifty-Five

Psalm 90:12

Lord, teach me to redeem the time I have on this earth. My days are truly numbered. May they be fashioned so as to continually glorify You.

Day Fifty-Six

John 14:27

O Lord, multiply Your peace in my life to the point that even in my own storms, I can bring Your calmness to bear upon the storms of others, especially to others who are placed in my care.

Day Fifty-Seven

I Samuel 3:10

Matthew 13:43

Lord, teach me the secret of a balance in prayer between listening and speaking. I am too oft interested more in speaking when I need to listen to You.

Day Fifty-Eight

John 17:5

I Corinthians 10:31

Lord, teach me the secret of not seeking my own glory, deliver me from the times my own pleasure or that of others is considered more important that what pleases You.

Day Fifty-Nine

Psalm 119:11

Matthew 5:44-45

Hide Your Word in my heart O God. Make Your way known through my actions. Help me to love those considered most unlovable in human terms.

Day Sixty

Acts 20:35

I John 3:16

Lord, remind me often that I am most like the Savior when I seek to give for the sake of others and to serve on behalf of all who are in need.

Day Sixty-One

I John 2:17

Ephesians 4:22-24

Make me, gracious Father, to know Your will in all things that I may go Your way and show Your way in the living of my life.

Day Sixty-Two

Psalm 46:10

Matthew 11:15

O, that I learn to listen to the silence, value the solitude, and bask in its worth. When my life is so loud and so busy, I can scarcely think, much less hear Your still, small whispers. Teach me the great benefit of being still and knowing You are God.

Day Sixty-Three

Luke 5:16; 10:38-42

Keep me back, O Lord, from
all that dries my spirit and
distracts me from following in the
way of the Savior.

Day Sixty-Four

Genesis 2:7

Acts 3:19-20

Breathe on me, Lord, the breath of Your Spirit, renew my whole life and empower me for the road that lies ahead.

Day Sixty-Five

Psalm 121:1-2

James 1:27

II Corinthians 9:8-9

Lord, give me a heart that both looks upward to You and outward to see the needs of those who are near yet at times seem far away.

Day Sixty-Six

Philippians 2:3-4

Guard my heart, O God, from times of such focus on my own needs, I scarcely, if at all, hear the cries of the needy.

Day Sixty-Seven

Luke 22:42

John 4:34

O, that I may learn the joy and victory of praying, "Not my will, but yours be done, Father" and not only say the words but live them out in every instance of my life.

Day Sixty-Eight

Psalm 22:19

James 4:8

Draw near to my heart, Lord God, especially in moments when I feel so far from You.

Day Sixty-Nine

I Corinthians 13:11

Father, may I seek nearness to You so that my childish ways become transformed into childlike ways.

Day Seventy

I Corinthians 12:3

Philippians 2:10-11

Lead me, dear Father, so that
when I say, "Jesus is Lord,"
he will be in every part of my life.

Day Seventy-One

Ephesians 4:32

Matthew 6:12-14

Help me design my response to others according to Your responses to me, Heavenly Father. Yours are always responses of grace.

Day Seventy-Two

Philippians 4:4

James 1:2-4

Lord, teach me to rejoice in You and all You have blessed me with, even when a challenge accompanies the blessing.

Day Seventy-Three

John 3:18

Acts 1:8

Teach me, Lord, that what matters most is believing all You have done for us through Jesus Christ. May I remember this in both times of solitude and when I am privileged to share with someone else.

Day Seventy-Four

Psalm 47:2; 73:25

O Lord, give me a heart which is so in awe of You that there is nothing either earthly or human that could ever compare with You. You are indeed an Awesome God.

Day Seventy-Five

Psalm 73:25-26

Help me graciously and joyfully bear scars from my association with Jesus Christ, even when they bring physical mistreatment.

Day Seventy-Six

Psalm 16:5; 94:17

Psalm 73:25-26

John 15:5

Help me avoid reaching a place where I fail to recognize just how much I need You and just how desperate I am without You.

Day Seventy-Seven

John 13:14-15

Mark 10:42-45

Give me, O God, the spirit of a servant which is so much like Jesus that I do not note any inconvenience as I serve in his name.

Day Seventy-Eight

Luke 23:46

II Peter 3:18

Help me grow in You, to the point where I can say as did Jesus, "Father, into your hands I commend my spirit," and truly mean it.

Day Seventy-Nine

Psalm 100:2

Matthew 6:24

Grant me Your grace, O God, so that surrender to Your Spirit becomes not a task or struggle but rather a consistent joy.

Day Eighty

Philippians 3:10-14

Hebrews 12:1-2

In the midst of all noise and distraction of life, I pray dear Lord that You grant me the ability to remain focused on Jesus Christ.

Day Eighty-One

Exodus 33:14

John 4:10

O Lord, I am reminded how very thirsty of soul I become and only Jesus Christ can give me living water.

Day Eighty-Two

Philippians 4:11

It is my desire, Lord, to become more and more thankful for Your presence and its meaning and become less complaining about what I desire more but which You reveal I need less.

Day Eighty-Three

Philippians 4:6-7

Grant to me, holy Father, a peace surpassing all human understanding so that while I may not fully comprehend its meaning, I always affirm Your peace in my heart.

Day Eighty-Four

Matthew 22:36-39

Lord, I confess slowness to love You completely, to love others as did Your Son, and to love myself as one named among Your redeemed. Forgive me, and lead me in the way everlasting.

Day Eighty-Five

Psalm 147:5

Jeremiah 31:3

In Your mighty presence, Lord
Jesus, I must shrink in humility,
yet You allow me to stand amazed
and secure in the firm grip of
Your love.

Day Eighty-Six

Ezekiel 36:26

Philippians 2:3-4

Grant, O Lord, my heart to become softened even in the face of hard things in life. May I be softened both by my challenges and by challenges in the lives of ones I love.

Day Eighty-Seven

II Corinthians 4:18

Lord, deliver me from a tendency to view earthly matters as permanent. Help me maintain proper perspective a vision of all that is eternal.

Day Eighty-Eight

John 4:34

Acts 4:19-20

Lord, remind me frequently that the world does not exist for my personal happiness or comfort. My life, my very being, exists to please You.

Day Eighty-Nine

Philippians 4:12-13

Help me never to choose an alternate path when the one on which You lead brings me to a rough part. Because I journey for You, help me bear with contentment all that exalts Christ, at any cost.

Day Ninety

John 3:21

I John 1:5

Lord, bring Your light to every corner of my life. Illumine me so that my life becomes a beacon and light for all who struggle with the darkness.

Day Ninety-One

Mark 6:12

Acts 19:11-12

Heal me, O God, that I may become instrumental in Your healing ministry. Let my healing and wholeness be nothing less than a showcase of Your grace.

Day Ninety-Two

Isaiah 6:8-9

Matthew 28:19-20

Help me be reminded, Lord Jesus, that the 'Go' in the Great Commission applies to me today just as it did on the day You said it. May I go to everyone to whom I am sent.

Day Ninety-Three

Luke 2:10

Mark 16:15

Empower me with such grace so as to empower me in sharing your good news with each person I meet. Luke 2:10 Mark 16:15

Day Ninety-Four

Luke 2:11

Romans 10:9

Lord, may the words, "Jesus is Lord," permeate me so much that others know that I belong to and serve the Master.

Day Ninety-Five

Matthew 15:8

II Corinthians 11:1

Have mercy on me, O Lord, for all the times I say I want to be more like Christ yet act less like him in my human dealings.

Day Ninety-Six

John 15:11

Hebrews 12:2

Truly, O Lord, Your joy is my strength, especially in times when joy generated from the world's perspective is greatly lacking.

Day Ninety-Seven

Matthew 6:6

Luke 18:1

Lord, make me ever more a person of prayer; not in speaking great words so much as communicating with You daily, moment by moment.

Day Ninety-Eight

Isaiah 12:3

II Corinthians 12:9

Matthew 7:24

Free me for joyful obedience Lord, so that what I do for you becomes my greatest pleasure and glorifies you.

Day Ninety-Nine

Psalm 104:33

Isaiah 12:2

Truly Jesus Christ is the song of my life. Thus I pray for a voice as long as I breathe which will sing the praises of my Savior.

Day One Hundred

II Corinthians 1:2

Romans 14:8

Revelation 14:13

May my days be so filled with Your welcome presence, Your grace, Your love, that when the sun sets on my time here, it is but a short distance to the place I will be with You forever. O Great God who meets all my needs, I love You, praise You, all my days here; as I await the time when I see You face to face.

These One Hundred Days are but a beginning. There will be more. There is always more; more we can receive and more we can return to the Lord. May each of you be overwhelmed and overjoyed, at the power and presence of Jesus Christ in your lives day by day. He is there at your every point of need. Blessed be his name, forever!

Curt